Tonka®
TRUCKS NIGHT AND DAY

by Patricia Relf
Illustrated by Thomas La Padula

Cartwheel
B·O·O·K·S®

SCHOLASTIC INC.
New York Toronto London Auckland Sydney
Mexico City New Delhi Hong Kong

Thank you to Lloyd Lambert and Ron Reid of the Kalamazoo County (Michigan) Road Commission; David Reed of the Kalamazoo/Battle Creek International Airport; David Littke of Wings Stadium in Kalamazoo; Pat Parker of Kalamazoo County Animal Control; Mike Cavey of American Hydrology; and everyone who patiently answered my truck questions. Special thanks to Emily Hanavan for research and writing help.

—P. R.

TONKA® and TONKA® logo are trademarks of Hasbro, Inc. Used with permission.
Copyright © 2000 by Hasbro, Inc. All rights reserved.
Published by Scholastic Inc., 555 Broadway, New York, NY 10012.
SCHOLASTIC, CARTWHEEL BOOKS and associated logos
are registered trademarks of Scholastic Inc.

ISBN 0-439-12196-5

Library of Congress Cataloging-in-Publication Data available

12 11 10 9 8 7 6 5 4 3 2 1   00 01 02 03 04

Printed in Singapore
First Scholastic printing, June 2000

Contents

Night Workers

While most people are sleeping, trucks are hard at work. An animal rescue truck picks up a lost dog. A grocery truck delivers boxes of food to a supermarket late at night after customers have left. A cherry picker lifts a worker high above the street to repair a cable television line. And trucks rush the first newspapers of the morning to stores and vending machines, ready for early risers.

Night Workers

NEWSPAPER TRUCK

Morning newspapers are actually printed in the middle of the night. Stacks of fresh papers are bundled together. If the weather is wet, the bundles are wrapped in plastic. Then a newspaper truck, called a drop hauler, delivers the bundles to stores and vending machines and carriers all over town. A carrier delivers one paper to each house on his or her route.

ANIMAL RESCUE TRUCK

Night and day, animal control officers rescue lost, dangerous, and injured animals. The rescue truck carries a capture pole for animals that are too dangerous or frightened to be picked up by hand. The snare or collar at the end of the capture pole can be tightened around an animal's neck. The truck carries stretchers for injured animals. Cats, puppies, and small wild animals such as raccoons or geese ride in the side compartments. Larger animals ride in one of the cages in the back.

CHERRY PICKER

A worker uses a cherry picker to reach a television cable high on a utility pole. She uses controls in the bucket to raise and lower herself. A worker on the ground can use a second set of controls on the truck in an emergency. The truck carries helmets, tools, lights, and rain gear— everything the crew needs to make repairs in all kinds of weather. A flashing light warns drivers to stay clear of the truck.

GROCERY TRUCK

Late at night, a grocery truck delivers cases of food to the supermarket. The big boxes are heavy, so workers slide the boxes along a rolling conveyor, a ramp with metal disks that spin. During the night, workers will unpack the boxes and put the cans on the store shelves, ready for shoppers to buy in the morning.

Many different trucks deliver food to supermarkets. The grocery truck delivers foods that come in cans and boxes and jars. A produce truck carries fruits and vegetables. A refrigerated truck brings frozen foods. Meat and dairy trucks are also refrigerated. A bakery truck delivers bread and cakes.

At the Ski Area

At a ski area, trucks work all night to be ready for morning visitors.
Powerful plows clear the roads so that drivers will be able to reach the
ski area safely. A front loader fills the plow trucks with a mixture of salt
and sand to spread on the roads. Snowcats carry workers to the top of the
mountain. An ice resurfacer cleans a skating rink for early-morning skaters.

At the Ski Area

ICE RESURFACER

An ice resurfacer, sometimes called a Zamboni machine, cleans and smooths an ice rink for skaters. Spinning brushes clean snow away from the edges of the rink. A sharp metal blade scrapes off the rough surface of the ice. Long screws called augers carry the ice scrapings up into the big tank. Another tank pours a little hot water onto the ice, and a towel drags behind, making the ice perfectly smooth. When the resurfacer finishes its job, its tank lifts like the back of a dump truck to empty out all the snow and bits of ice.

SNOWCAT

The powerful engine and wide tracks of a snowcat let it climb up steep, slippery slopes and across fresh snow. The snowcat carries workers and food to the lodge at the top of the mountain, and it carries skiers to remote parts of the mountain where the snow is fresh and powdery. Closer to the lodge, it packs the snow down to make a smooth, firm path for skiing. In an emergency, the snowcat can carry an injured person to safety.

FRONT LOADER

At the garage, a small but powerful loader scoops up salt and sand from enormous piles and mixes them together. Then it dumps the mixture into the back of the snowplow truck. The loader can move piles of snow, and, in the summer, it can scoop and carry dirt and rocks. The driver controls the bucket by moving levers in the cab.

SNOWPLOW

The plow's long blade pushes snow to the side of the road, leaving a clear path for drivers. The truck carries a mixture of salt, to help melt ice, and sand, to make the road less slippery. At the back of the truck, a long screw churns salt and sand into a hole, where it drops down onto a spinning wheel. The wheel scatters the mixture all over the road. A computer in the truck makes sure that just the right amount of salt and sand is dispensed.

A snowplow blade is made of carbon steel, a very hard metal. Even so, scraping against roads all day wears the blade down. After only a week or so, it must be replaced with a new blade.

On the Farm

By the time day breaks, farmers are hard at work. They have already milked the cows. The fresh milk is pumped into a tanker truck which will take it to a dairy to be bottled. Today, a cattle transport is taking some of the cattle to a different farm. Tractors pull special farm machines through the fields. At the end of winter, one machine spreads manure on the ground to help the corn grow in the spring. A seed drill pokes holes in the ground and drops a seed in each hole.

On the Farm

MANURE SPREADER

Adding manure to the soil will help the corn grow in the spring. A tractor pulls a manure spreader through the fields. Chains whirl inside the spreader, throwing the manure evenly across the field. Manure is made from animal waste and straw that is cleaned out of the barn each day.

SEED DRILL

When it is time to plant corn, the farmer fills the seed drill with seed corn. Then a tractor pulls the drill through the fields. Sharp blades poke holes in the soil and drop one seed into each hole. Metal rods push dirt back into the holes. The farmer waits for rain and sun, and soon corn plants will be growing in neat rows. This corn is not for people; the whole plant will be chopped up to make food for the farm animals.

CATTLE TRANSPORT

When cattle are sold to another farm or taken to the fair, they ride in a cattle transport truck. The cattle climb up a ramp and stand in stalls. Holes in the walls of the trailer allow fresh air in.

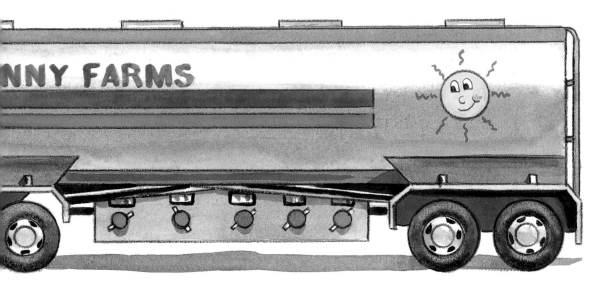

MILK TANKER

A milk tanker travels to dairy farms collecting milk. The driver attaches a hose to the farmer's tank and pumps the fresh milk into the tanker truck. The milk goes to a dairy, where it will be pasteurized—that is, heated to kill germs—and bottled.

The driver of a milk tanker takes a small sample of each farm's milk and measures how much butterfat it contains. The more butterfat in the milk, the more butter, cream, and ice cream it can make. Milk with more butterfat is worth more money.

16

Moving Day

People often move to a new house...but sometimes the house itself moves to a new spot! This house is moving to make way for a road. It rides on steel beams with wheels attached. A wrecking crane knocks down the old foundation and a garden wall. A bulldozer pushes rocks, old cement, and earth to make the ground flat for the new road. A tree mover digs up a tree and carries it to a new place, too.

Moving Day

BULLDOZER

A powerful bulldozer pushes rocks and dirt to level the land. Crawler tracks carry the bulldozer over rough or soft ground. Hydraulic rams raise, lower, and turn the blade.

WRECKING CRANE

A wrecking crane knocks walls down quickly. The crane's long arm, or jib, can be raised or lowered. A wrecking ball hangs from the end of the jib by a cable. The operator uses a dragline to pull the wrecking ball back . . . and then lets it go. The wrecking ball swings into the wall, knocking it down with a crash.

TREE MOVER

Instead of cutting down a tree, why not move it? A tree mover's enormous blades dig into the earth around a tree. The blades cut a huge cone of soil that includes the largest of the tree's roots. The tree mover carries the entire tree and its roots and plants it in a new spot.

HOUSE MOVER

To move a whole house, workers prepare for weeks beforehand. They disconnect electrical wires and water pipes. They cut holes in the house's foundation. They push steel beams under the house in both directions. Workers lift up the house using hydraulic jacks and then attach wheels under the beams. At last it is moving day. The workers connect the beams to a tractor, the kind that would usually pull a semitrailer. Very slowly, the house rolls away to its new location.

When a house moves down a road, workers must take down the overhead wires along the way—all of the telephone, electricity, and cable television wires. Tree trimmers cut away overhanging branches. Police cars drive ahead to stop traffic on the road.

Road Workers

Day and night, trucks are busy making roads safer. A pavement-patching truck fills
holes in the road. Line-painting trucks paint the white and yellow lines that show
drivers where to drive. A sign truck replaces a stop sign. Workers trim tree branches
so that buses and trucks can drive underneath, and a chipper chops the branches
into small pieces.

Road Workers

SIGN TRUCK

After a careless driver hits a stop sign, the sign must be replaced right away. At the front of a sign truck, a hydraulic lift pulls the old signpost out of the ground. The truck carries new posts and signs. A hydraulic hammer at the back of the truck pounds a new post into the ground, and workers bolt a new sign onto it. Now everyone will know that they must stop here.

PAVEMENT PATCHER

A pavement-patching truck carries a load of hot, black asphalt. A conveyor belt rolls the fresh asphalt out of the back of the truck. A spray of oily liquid made from corn helps to keep the gooey asphalt from sticking to the truck. Workers use shovels to push the asphalt into holes.

CHIPPER

When tree branches hang into the street, workers use chain saws to trim them. They throw the branches into the back of a big chipper pulled by a dump truck. The chipper's sharp, fast-moving blades pull the branches in and chop them to pieces. The chipper shoots the pieces into the truck in front. The truck dumps the chips at a park or garden. The wood chips make wonderful mulch, a coating for the ground around trees and bushes. Mulch helps to keep weeds from growing, keeps water in the ground, and looks pretty, too.

LINE PAINTER

Yellow and white lines on the road show drivers where to drive. A line-painting machine sprays special heated paint onto the road. Tiny bits of glass mixed in the paint make the lines shiny at night. A warning truck follows behind the line painter to prevent cars from driving on the wet paint. In less than a minute, the paint is dry.

What do the lines on a road mean? A solid line in the center tells drivers not to pass another car because a curve or hill makes it difficult to see cars coming from the opposite direction. A broken line means that cars may pass each other if it is safe.

On the Highway

Highways are busy at every time of day. A race car transporter carries cars to their next race at a faraway track. An armored truck delivers money safely to the bank. A double semitrailer carries twice as much as an ordinary truck. And a bookmobile, like a library on wheels, hurries to its next stop.

On the Highway

ARMORED TRUCK

Very valuable things, such as money and jewels, can be carried safely inside an armored truck. The truck itself is made of specially strong armored steel. The glass is bulletproof. The side and back doors can be opened only if the driver unlocks them from inside the truck and uses a key, too. Corner mirrors let the driver check behind the truck for robbers. Small openings, called gun ports, all over the truck, are just big enough for the driver to shoot through if the truck were attacked.

DOUBLE SEMITRAILER

The front section of a semitrailer is called the tractor because its powerful engine does the pulling. Some tractors can pull two trailers, carrying nearly twice as much as a single rig. The second trailer is connected to the first with a dolly, which acts as front wheels for the second trailer. Then the driver plugs in electrical cords and air tubes which work the lights and brakes on the two trailers.

RACE CAR CARRIER

A special semitrailer carries race cars to tracks all over the country. A platform at the back of the trailer lifts cars to the upper level. The truck also serves as a repair shop. It carries all of the spare parts and tools needed to fix the cars.

BOOKMOBILE

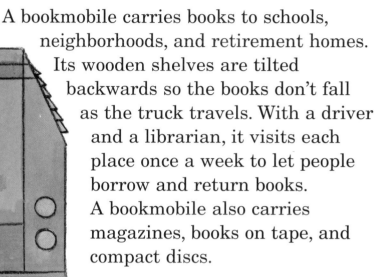

A bookmobile carries books to schools, neighborhoods, and retirement homes. Its wooden shelves are tilted backwards so the books don't fall as the truck travels. With a driver and a librarian, it visits each place once a week to let people borrow and return books. A bookmobile also carries magazines, books on tape, and compact discs.

Look closely at a semitrailer. Two tubes run from the tractor to each trailer. These tubes send air to the brakes, causing the brakes to slow or stop the truck. The main air line, called the service line, is usually colored blue. The emergency line is red; it works in case the main line does not.

At a Festival

It's almost time for a concert! The performers come from far away, so they ride together in a fancy, customized bus. A catering truck brings food for all the performers and their crew. The concert will appear on television, so a live-television truck is ready to send pictures and sound signals back to the studio. A trash hauler empties the stadium's big trash container.

At a Festival

CUSTOMIZED BUS

Performers who travel long distances ride in special buses to make their trips more comfortable. This bus is like a mobile home, with beds, a sitting area, a small kitchen, and even a bathroom. After the show, the musicians can sleep or watch television while the driver takes them to the next city.

CATERING TRUCK

Caterers prepare food in their own kitchens, then serve the food wherever it is needed. This truck has small warming ovens to keep the hot food hot, and there are coolers for cold food. Special cases hold dishes and silverware. A crew of workers unloads the food and helps to serve guests.

LIVE-TELEVISION TRUCK

A live-television truck sends pictures and sound from just about anywhere back to the television studio. The engineer parks the truck and raises the tall mast. The dish at the top sends signals back to the studio. The engineer uses a radio to talk to workers at the television studio and adjusts the signal to make the sound and picture just right. Now thousands of people can see the same concert or news event on television, at the very time it happens.

TRASH HAULER

Big stores, restaurants, and stadiums create a lot of trash. The bags of trash go outside into a large metal container. When the container is full, a trash hauler empties it. Two forks pick up the container and lift it up and over the truck. The container flips upside down, its lid flops open, and the trash falls into the truck. Inside the truck, a big blade pushes the trash toward the back.

Where does trash go? Trucks dump most trash at landfills, huge areas where garbage piles up and up. Eventually, the pile will be covered with dirt and planted with trees or grass. Some old landfills are now parks or even ski areas!

Airport Trucks

All day and all night, airplanes take off and land at the airport. That means that airport trucks are busy all the time, too. A small tractor pulls a baggage cart loaded with suitcases, trunks—and even a dog carrier. A fuel truck fills up an airliner's tanks before it takes off. In cold, snowy weather, a de-icing truck sprays each airplane to remove ice. If a pilot reports a problem before landing, a fire truck stands ready, just in case.

Airport Trucks

DE-ICING TRUCK

An airplane that is covered with ice may have trouble flying. So, if the weather is cold and wet, a de-icing truck parks beside the plane just before it takes off. The truck has a heater which warms up de-icing liquid. Then it sprays the hot liquid, called glycol, through a hose. When the ice is gone, the de-icing truck drives away and the plane can take off safely.

FIRE TRUCK

An airport fire truck has special nozzles, called roof turrets, that can shoot water, foam, or dry, powdered chemicals at a fire from far away. Foam puts out fuel fires. Dry chemicals must be used to put out fires in certain parts of airplanes. The truck's floodlights light up the scene of an accident. The truck carries tools called "jaws of life" which can cut through metal and hold the gap open while rescue workers reach an injured person.

BAGGAGE TRUCK

A small tractor called a tug can pull one baggage cart or a whole train of them. Suitcases, boxes, golf bags, musical instruments, and pet carriers all ride from the terminal to the airplane on the baggage truck. Plastic flaps protect the baggage from rain and snow.

FUEL TRUCK

An airplane cannot drive to a gas station, so a fuel truck brings fuel to the airplane. Like a pump at the gas station, the truck has a pump that measures how much fuel the airplane takes. The pilot needs to know exactly how much fuel is on board so that she can figure out how much the airplane weighs for takeoff.

Air traffic controllers, working in the airport's tower, make sure that every airplane has room to take off and land safely. Every ground vehicle at an airport has a radio, and drivers must get permission from the air traffic controllers before they drive anywhere planes might go.